BRITAIN IN OLD PHOTOGRAPHS

TWICKENHAM, TEDDINGTON & HAMPTON

MIKE CHERRY, KEN HOWE & JOHN SHEAF

SUTTON PUBLISHING LIMITED

Sutton Publishing Limited
Phoenix Mill · Thrupp · Stroud
Gloucestershire · GL5 2BU

First published 1996
Reprinted 1997

Copyright © Mike Cherry, Ken Howe
and John Sheaf, 1996

Title page photograph: The Hotel, Eel Pie Island,
from the Embankment, early 1900s.

British Library Cataloguing in Publication Data
A catalogue record for this book is available from the
British Library.

ISBN 0-7509-1110-7

Typeset in 10/12 Perpetua.
Typesetting and origination by
Sutton Publishing Limited.
Printed in Great Britain by
Ebenezer Baylis, Worcester.

ABOUT THE AUTHORS

Mike Cherry, Ken Howe and John Sheaf are very good friends who live in Twickenham, Teddington and Hampton respectively. They are all prominent members of the Borough of Twickenham Local History Society and participate fully in all its activities. They are authors, individually or jointly, of a number of books on local history including *Hampton and Teddington Past, Teddington Past and Present* and *Hampton in the 1890s – Through the Eyes of Captain Christie of Beveree*, pamphlets, papers and articles and give talks on various aspects of the area described in this book.

In addition, they are all founder members of the West London Postcard Club and have large collections of old photographs and postcards of their areas. They have collected this material for more than a decade and have selected some of the very best items to illustrate this book. Many of these pictures are rare, some unique, and nearly all have never been published in book form before.

The authors are also members of their local societies and amenity groups, and all take a great interest in the locality, its history and development, and in the preservation of the best of the past. They are particularly keen to broaden people's interest in the community and history of the area covered in the book and hope that it will encourage a greater awareness in, and knowledge of, the locality.

Readers who share some or all of the interests mentioned are encouraged to join the Borough of Twickenham Local History Society (which covers the Hamptons, Teddington and Whitton as well as Twickenham). The annual subscription is £6.00 and should be sent to the Membership Secretary, 86 Cole Park Road, Twickenham TW1 1JA.

CONTENTS

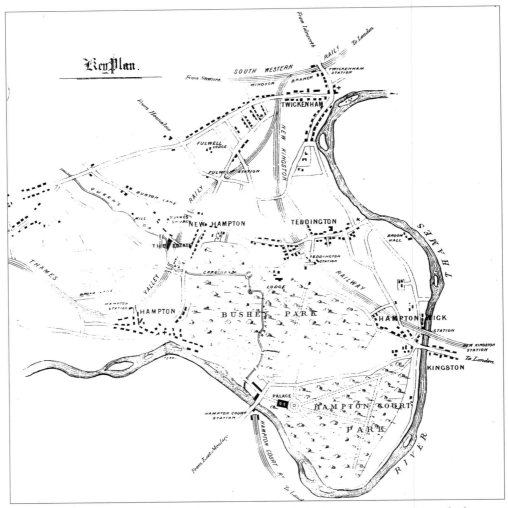

This map dates from *c.* 1868 and shows the area covered in the book as it was at approximately the time of the earliest photographs published here. Readers will be only too aware of the enormous development that has taken place since.

INTRODUCTION

Rapid and far-reaching changes in nineteenth-century society gave rise to the old Borough of Twickenham that is the subject area of this book. During the same period the invention of photography created a new and vivid way of recording the lives of the local people which has made the book possible.

The nineteenth century brought a mass of legislation aimed at improving the lot of the working classes such as the 1819 Act to amend the Laws for the Relief of the Poor, the 1834 Poor Law Amendment Act and the 1848 Public Health Act. At the same time, transport was becoming more available and cheaper with the main coach routes well established and the railways network starting to spread across the country. The combined effect of these advances was to place a greater administrative burden on the parish vestries of the land. Up until then they were the local government of the day, appointing churchwardens, constables, overseers and surveyors. Religious tolerance was also chipping away at the established order – ratepayers who were not members of the Church of England parish church now demanded a say in their community affairs. The result of these factors was the Local Government Act of 1858, 'an Act which gave authority for the formation of Local Boards to be responsible for local affairs'.

Hampton Wick passed a resolution in favour of forming a local board at their first meeting in 1863; Teddington voted against it in 1864 but subsequently elected for it after a Home Office inquiry in 1867; Twickenham residents were for it at their first meeting in 1867, but Hampton argued against it from 1865 to 1890 and only then formed a board after the Middlesex County Council made an order for the conversion of Hampton into an urban district. The four local boards later became urban district councils and in 1937 they were combined to become the Borough of Twickenham.

The nineteenth century also saw the invention of photography (accredited to the year 1827), and by the 1860s commercial photographers were springing up all over the country. Later, apart from dealing with portrait photography, they supplemented their incomes by creating picture postcards of their local areas, a practice permitted by the Post Office from September 1894.

This venture proved very popular with the general public who took to sending cards in rather the same fashion that we now use the telephone; they proved a cheap and quick way of keeping in touch with relatives and friends. Fortunately this predilection has supplied us with a remarkable record of social history, noting the changes in fashion and transport and providing a definitive record of many of the fine old houses of the day that have now disappeared.

In this book, we have drawn mainly on our own collections of postcards, the majority of which have not been previously published, to give a view of what became the old Borough of Twickenham. While every effort has been made to ensure that the captions are factually accurate, in the event of any errors having crept in, we would be pleased to receive any corrections or indeed any additional information.

Mike Cherry
Ken Howe
John Sheaf
1996

Park Road, Teddington, c. 1863. This was shortly after the bridge had been built and shows J. Reed's grocer's shop on the left with the Clarence Hotel behind. It is one of the oldest photographs of Teddington.

CENTRAL AND NORTH TWICKENHAM

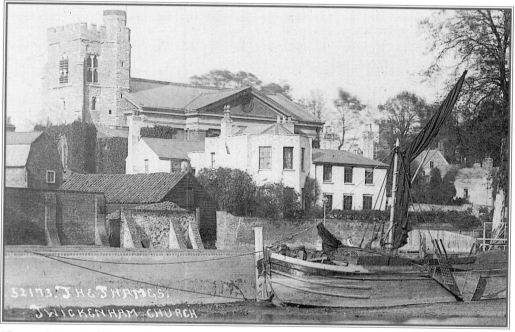

The parish church of St Mary the Virgin, early 1890s. The nave was rebuilt in 1715, but the church retains its medieval tower of Kentish ragstone. The painter Sir Godfrey Kneller, who lived at Kneller Hall in Whitton, was a churchwarden at the time the nave was rebuilt. The vicarage in the foreground was demolished in the mid-1890s and Dial House to the far right was given to the parish as a replacement by Elizabeth Twining, a local benefactress.

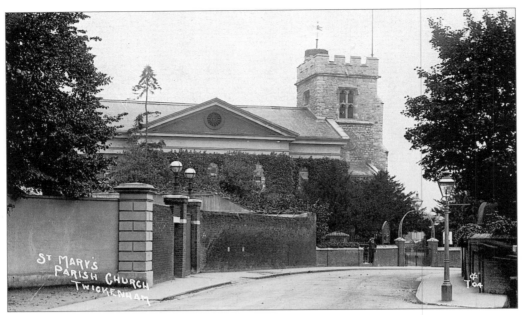

St Mary's Church, *c.* 1910 with Church Street in the foreground.

Horse-drawn delivery cart of T.L. Morris's bakery, *c.* 1895.

Group photograph taken in the stabling at the rear of Morris's Baker's Shop, No. 14 Church Street, *c.* 1895. Thomas Laban Morris, the proprietor, is the bearded figure; in front of him is his younger son Laban, and on Laban's left sits John Morris, Thomas Laban's elder son and successor.

Church Street, at the junction with Water Lane and King Street, *c*. 1910. With the construction of York Street in 1899, Church Street ceased to be the main route through Twickenham to Richmond, but it retained its importance as the commercial centre of the town with a rich variety of businesses, from staymaker to undertaker. At the date of this photograph, there were 42 traders in the street. This total included 4 butchers, 3 bootmakers, 3 dining rooms, and 2 each of fishmongers, grocers, bakers, and outfitters (including William Henry Stapleton's large shop on the right).

Church Street, in a view looking west, *c*. 1911.

Members of the Borough of Twickenham Local History Society led by Miss R. Sanford (on the extreme right) begin excavation of part of the car park in Church Street, Easter 1966. The photograph shows one of the six trenches, each 8 feet square, which were dug on the site. Finds included prehistoric bones, Neolithic flints, and potsherds dating from the Neolithic period to the eighteenth century.

Arragon Tower, Church Street, was the remaining part of Twickenham Manor House, a Tudor building with later additions. The name derives from an unfounded tradition that Catherine of Aragon was connected with the manor. Most of the house was demolished in the 1860s, the tower remaining until 1934 when it was dismantled and the Tudor bricks were taken for use at Hampton Court.

Water Lane in a view looking towards the Thames with Eel Pie Island in the distance. The military uniforms suggest that this photograph dates from the First World War. The premises on the left are Leigh and Sons, plumbers and gas fitters.

Bell Lane, *c.* 1900. Like Water Lane, Bell Lane was one of several roads leading to the riverside from Church Street, and they comprised some of the oldest and most densely populated parts of Twickenham. Many of the buildings in this picture were destroyed by bombing in the Second World War.

Shore's Boat House at the end of Water Lane in the early 1900s viewed from Eel Pie Island. Charlie Shore was a well-known Twickenham waterman who had founded the Boys' and Girls' Regatta in 1894. He died in 1916.

A dense crowd of spectators on Twickenham Embankment in front of Shore's Boat House watching the Boys' and Girls' Regatta in the early 1900s. Apart from rowing, this very popular annual event included sideshows, fireworks and contests such as climbing the greasy pole.

Eel Pie Island viewed from the tower of St Mary's Church, *c.* 1922. Apart from the boatbuilders and the hotel, the island was largely undeveloped. At the bottom right of the picture is the Barmy Arms a seventeenth-century inn formerly known as the Queen's Head.

The Hotel, Eel Pie Island, *c.* 1910. Constructed in 1830 to replace an earlier and much more modest inn called the White Cross (described as a 'dingy wooden cottage'), the hotel traded on the island's reputation as a place of leisure and pleasure. Celebrated by Charles Dickens in *Nicholas Nickleby* (published in 1838 at a time when Dickens was living in Twickenham), the hotel was a favourite resort for boating parties and day trippers, some of whom are shown here being entertained by a singer on the balcony. The hotel was finally demolished in 1971 after a brief period as a jazz, rock and blues venue.

King Street in the early 1900s. The Twickenham Meat Market with its splendid display of carcasses is on the corner of Queen's Road and was owned by Ernest Skull, a butcher who also had premises at No. 29 King Street and No. 50 Church Street. The buildings together with the George Inn remain but much of the rest of King Street has since been redeveloped.

The south side of King Street, *c.* 1904. The town hall to the right was built in 1877 by Sir Charles Freake, a property developer who was living at Fulwell Park, and housed Twickenham's first public library from 1882. The King's Head Hotel (left) was established in 1747 and, like the George Inn on the other side of the road, had extensive stabling at the rear to cater for the coach trade through King Street. The whole of the south side frontage was demolished in 1926 to allow for road widening.

King Street, *c.* 1912, showing to the right the wall of Richmond House (now the site of the disused swimming pool) and the old town hall. Of particular interest on the left is the Twickenham Picture Palace, the first permanent cinema in Twickenham, which operated from 1910 to 1914. It was converted from a shop, and behind an ornate plasterwork frontage had a 300-seat auditorium. The building now houses the Oxfam shop.

King Street in a view looking towards the junction with Heath Road and Cross Deep taken *c.* 1930s. The Luxor cinema opened in 1929 and was designed in the Egyptian style. It was renamed the Odeon in 1944 and closed in 1981.

The Horse and Groom public house on the north side of King Street in the early 1900s. This building stood on the site of an earlier inn of the same name; licensing records for Twickenham refer to 'Horse and Groom' from at least 1749. Demolished in the mid-1930s, its ground now forms part of the site of Woolworths. To the immediate right of the building is the passageway which still runs from King Street to Holly Road.

Interior view of the Horse and Groom contemporary with the previous photograph. Note the model of a horse and groom suspended from the ceiling.

Construction of tramlines in London Road, 1902; those to the left go to Isleworth, those curving to the right along York Street to Richmond. A number of old buildings were demolished to allow for road widening.

Tramway construction further down London Road, 3 July 1902. The entrance to Grosvenor Road can be seen to the left. Note the sober clothing of the navvies with their waistcoats and ubiquitous cloth caps.

This photograph, taken in 1912, shows the junction of London Road (to the left) with York Street which was opened on 1 March 1899. A celebration dinner was held on that day at the Albany Hotel, Station Yard.

Twickenham Police Station, London Road, in 1908. The building is shown on the 1863 Ordnance Survey map although the freehold of the property was only bought by the Metropolitan Police Receiver in 1902, having previously been leased. The site was extended in 1919 by the purchase of Nos 86 and 88 Grosvenor Road from George Mesley, and in the following year thirteen cottages (Nos 60 to 84 Grosvenor Road) were purchased to allow for further building. The gates to the left of the picture are of Musgrave and Co.'s Amyand Park Dairy.

Interior view of Fortescue House, *c*. 1900. The building was used as a Shaftesbury Home from 1878 until 1937 when it was demolished. The last cinema to be built in Twickenham, the Regal, opened on the site on 9 October 1939 and was replaced by Regal House in 1960.

Fortescue House, London Road, *c*. 1915. Named after an eighteenth-century owner, Earl Fortescue, the building was used for educational purposes for much of its life – as Miss Dutton's Female Boarding School in the early nineteenth century (where Mary Shelley née Wollstonecraft was believed to have been a pupil) and as the Metropolitan and City Police Orphanage from 1870 to 1874.

London Road in a view looking south towards the town centre photographed *c.* 1912. The Railway Tavern (now the Cabbage Patch) is on the right, and the entrance to Arragon Road (then Amyand Park Road) to the left.

Twickenham Station, *c.* 1950. The station had opened in 1848 when the railway was extended west from Richmond to Windsor. The houses and engine shed to the right still stand but the station was rebuilt on the east side of Cole's Bridge in 1954.

Whitton Road, *c.* 1915. Chase Bridge over the River Crane is in the far distance; the houses on the right back on to the rugby ground which at the date of this photograph was a modest stadium with one covered grandstand.

The rugby ground in use for an assembly of Jehovah's Witnesses, July 1963. Note the tented village at the top right of the picture.

York House in the early 1900s in a view taken from the front; the portico on the main entrance was later removed. Since 1926 York House has been the Borough Council's offices, initially for the Borough of Twickenham and, since 1965, for the enlarged Borough of Richmond upon Thames. Much altered and extended over the centuries, the original house was built in the early 1600s and is probably the building shown under construction on Moses Glover's map of 1635. Subsequent occupants included the Earl of Clarendon who was Lord Chancellor to Charles II, the Comte de Paris and the Duc d'Orléans in the nineteenth century; from 1906 the last private owner was Sir Ratan Tata the Indian industrialist.

Installed in 1909 by Sir Ratan Tata as part of his improvements to his York House estate, the statues of sea nymphs and horses are of Italian marble and are thought to have been carved by Italian craftsmen, although their origin is still uncertain. They were acquired from Lea Park near Godalming.

Rustic bridge, Riverside, c. 1909. This wooden bridge was built in the 1890s as part of the Duc d'Orléans' extensive changes to the York House estate. The bridge provided access to the gardens which he had created by building a high wall around the riverside meadows, in the face of much local opposition.

Richmond Road looking towards York Street, c. 1950. The Gaumont cinema had opened in 1928 as the Twickenham Kinema, seating 1,200. It was renamed the Queens in 1940 but closed shortly afterwards and the site was leased to the council as a furniture store. It was sold to Odeon Theatres in 1944 and reopened, changing its name to the Gaumont in 1949. The buildings on the left were redeveloped in the 1980s as the Borough's new Civic Centre with the Edwardian façade retained.

St John's Hospital, Amyand Park Road, *c.* 1915. The hospital was founded by Elizabeth Twining, who purchased the eighteenth-century Amyand House in 1879 for the purpose. Opened in 1880, the hospital closed in 1883 for financial reasons, re-opening in 1885 and continuing to provide local cottage hospital services until 1988. The site has since been redeveloped as a psychogeriatric hospital and Amyand House refurbished. An excavation on the site in 1994 prior to new building revealed the most substantial evidence so far of Roman settlement in Twickenham.

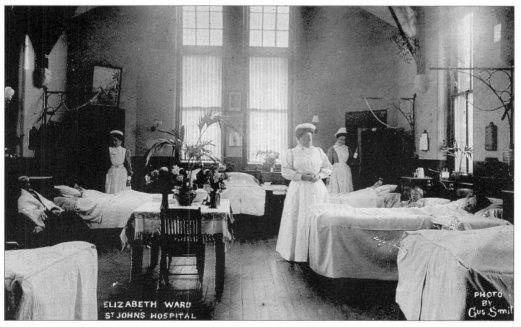

Elizabeth Ward, St John's Hospital, *c.* 1908. Sister Agnes Edginton, standing right of centre, had been a member of Elizabeth Twining's household at whose expense she trained as a nurse.

Twickenham Ferry and Riverside, c. 1927. Much of this view is little changed from the eighteenth century when Ferryside, Ferry House, the White Swan, and other buildings on Riverside were built. Mount Lebanon on the far right, shown here for sale, replaced an earlier house, and was destroyed by fire in 1909.

Twickenham Ferry, c. 1909. Ferry Cottage on the left was built at the turn of the century by Lord Dysart, owner of the ferry, for William Champion the ferryman. The wooden hut on the Petersham bank was erected at about the same time to enable the ferryman's wife to sell refreshments. The ferry was celebrated in 1878 in a very popular river ditty by Theo Marzials called 'Twickenham Ferry'; thirty-five years later the ferry again achieved fame when Lord Dysart and William Champion brought an action against Walter Hammerton who had set up a ferry in competition by Marble Hill Park. Hammerton ultimately won the action. Twickenham Ferry ceased trading in recent years.

EAST TWICKENHAM AND MARBLE HILL

Marble Hill House. The condition of the house suggests that this view dates from soon after 1903 when the estate was saved from demolition and housing development by the London County Council which bought the property and opened the park and house to the public. The house, built between 1724 and 1728 for Henrietta Howard, Countess of Suffolk and mistress of George II, has gradually been restored.

The Clock House, Marble Hill Park, *c.* 1907. The Clock House was built as a stable block for the Marble Hill House estate in 1825–7 by Jonathan, later General, Peel, who was a politician and soldier and who lived at Marble Hill House from 1825 to 1879. These stables replaced the original block which stood approximately on the site of the present car park.

Twickenham residents at play in Marble Hill Park, *c.* 1911. The park quickly established itself as a popular place for leisure and sport with tennis courts and a cricket pitch laid out in the grounds.

Montpelier Chapel, Chapel Road, between Montpelier Row and Orleans Road. The chapel was built in the 1720s by Captain Gray who had also built Montpelier Row. It ceased to function as a chapel after St Stephen's Church was constructed and in later years was an accumulator factory and a laundry. Unused after 1930, the building finally collapsed in 1941.

The Crown Public House, Richmond Road, in a photograph probably dating from the early 1890s. The sign to the right bears the name Williams, a family associated with the Crown since 1866 when John Williams became landlord; he was succeeded by his son Arthur in 1895.

Highshot House, *c.* 1907. Built in the late eighteenth century, Highshot House stood at the junction of Crown and Richmond Roads. From 1800 to 1807 it was home to Louis Philippe Duc d'Orléans and his brothers Antoine Duc de Montpensier and Charles Comte de Beaujolais during their exile from France. From 1885 until 1909 the house served as a retreat for gentlemen inebriates, and subsequently as a surgical appliance factory until its demolition in 1927. Only the doorway was retained and incorporated into the new building on the site.

Celebrations and the procession in Crown Road on Charter Day, 22 September 1926, when Twickenham acquired the status of a municipal borough instead of an urban district.

A view of Amyand Park Road, looking towards Crown Road, taken in the early 1900s. St Margaret's Station is on the left.

St Margaret's Hotel at the junction of St Margaret's and Crown Roads, *c.* 1917.

St Margaret's Station, *c.* 1911. The station opened in October 1876. Note the steam traction engine in the background.

The Broadway, St Margaret's, in a view looking towards the station taken in the early 1900s.

Aerial view of Cambridge Park in 1928; Richmond Bridge is to the right and Cambridge House is on the left. In the foreground between the factory buildings and the river is the Sports-Drome under construction. It opened on 18 December 1928 as an ice rink with a skating surface measuring 286 feet by 80 feet but was financially unsuccessful and closed in 1932. The rink was redesigned and re-opened in 1934, finally closing in 1992. Luxury housing now occupies the site.

Cambridge House viewed from Cambridge Road, *c.* 1910. Originally an imposing Jacobean mansion built in about 1616 by Sir Humphrey Lind, Cambridge House took its name from Richard Owen Cambridge who owned the estate in the second half of the eighteenth century. The house was substantially altered in the nineteenth century by Henry Bevan. However, by 1910 most of the 74 acres of parkland had been developed for housing and Cambridge House was increasingly hemmed in by homes and factories. It was demolished in 1937.

Jersey cows grazing at Home Farm. Now the site of Beresford Avenue, the farm was owned by Josiah Clarke who had moved there from Richmond in 1908. The firm of J. Clarke & Sons, later Hornby and Clarke, was subsequently taken over by the Express Dairy.

The Avenue, St Margaret's, *c.* 1906. Several of the large houses on the left of this photograph were demolished with the construction in 1933 of Twickenham Bridge and its approach road which runs parallel to The Avenue.

Twickenham Park Mews, *c.* 1905. Twickenham Park was probably created soon after 1227 when Richard, Earl of Cornwall became lord of the manor. At the date of this photograph much of the park had already been sold for development, and Twickenham Park House, built in the 1820s (a successor to at least two earlier substantial houses), was sold and demolished in 1928 to allow for the final phase of house building. A sale catalogue of 1908 shows three possible locations for the mews, the most likely being just west of the junction of Arlington Road and Arlington Mews.

This photograph of 1928 shows the remains of the ha-ha between Twickenham Park House and Duck's Walk, and the half-excavated gravel pit surrounding the house. The building was demolished in 1929.

Aerial view of the Chertsey Road in the early 1930s. The gravel pit in the previous picture has been filled in and Twickenham Bridge, which opened in 1933, and the Chertsey Road are complete.

The Royal Naval School, St Margaret's, *c.* 1918. Founded in 1840 at Hope House, Little Green, Richmond and originally called the Royal Naval Female School for 'educating at a reduced cost to parents the daughters of necessetous naval and marine officers', the school moved in 1856 to St Margaret's House which had been built in 1851 by the 2nd Earl of Kilmorey. The school remained at St Margaret's House until 1940 when the building was virtually destroyed by bombing.

Pupils in the grounds of the Royal Naval School, St Margaret's.

Thomas Chandler Haliburton (1796–1865), in an early photograph, *c.* 1860. He became a judge and author (both of the satirical 'Sam Slick' essays and of historical and political works) in Nova Scotia. Settling in England in 1856, he lived in Gordon House until his death in 1865. He was elected MP for Launceston in 1859. Haliburton is shown here reading in a room in Gordon House; some of the furniture in the picture is now in the hands of his descendants. The house, which still stands and is now part of Brunel University, is part seventeenth century and was much enlarged by Moses Hart in the early eighteenth century. A small wing was added for the next owner, General Humphry Bland, in 1758, by Robert Adam (his first building in England).

STRAWBERRY HILL

Poulett Lodge, built in 1734 by Dr William Battie, President of the Royal College of Physicians, was owned from 1758 by Vere Poulett (later the 3rd Earl Poulett) after whom the house was named, and in whose family's possession it remained until 1870. The house was altered in the late nineteenth century and after brief use as a club, the riverside building was demolished and replaced by Thames Eyot flats.

A view of Pope's Villa, Cross Deep, in the centre, *c.* 1918. It was built in 1842 by Thomas Young, a tea merchant, on the approximate site of Pope's original house. The building to the left, the right half of which remains as Ryan House, was built by Baroness Howe who in 1807 had bought and then demolished Alexander Pope's original (although extended) house.

THE CHILD
MOSES
Leaving to Heaven.

Entrance to
Pope's Grotto. 1676.

Bust of
Pope.

Little Tich
Removed from the
Tower of London

Entrance to Pope's Grotto, early 1900s. In order to provide access from his riverside villa to his gardens on the other side of Cross Deep, Pope had a tunnel constructed which he decorated with shells, glass, marble, lava and other exotic materials. The tunnel still exists but the decoration was stripped away in the early 1800s by Baroness Howe.

St Catherine's Convent School, *c.* 1923. The school moved to Pope's Villa in 1919 from Orford Lodge in Pope's Grove, having been founded in 1914 in a house called St Catherine's in Vicarage Road.

The senior classroom of St Catherine's School in the 1920s.

Cross Deep Hall gardens and boathouse in the early 1900s. Cross Deep Hall stood on the riverside of Cross Deep approximately opposite the Pope's Grotto public house and Holmes Road. The house is thought to have been built in the eighteenth century for Samuel Scott the painter. A 1928 sale catalogue refers to the 'ornamental boathouse over which is a picturesque tea house'.

Tower Road in a view looking towards the river taken in the 1920s. The water tower on the right was built by Lady Waldegrave in the nineteenth century to supply water to Strawberry Hill. It was taken down in 1950.

Radnor House seen from the riverside, *c.* 1920. The house stood next to Cross Deep Hall and took its name from John Robartes, 4th Earl of Radnor who lived there from 1722 until his death in 1757. The original house was probably built in 1673 but it was much extended and altered by successive owners. The earliest prints, dating from 1750, show the house with a Gothic appearance, and in the 1840s William Chillingworth remodelled it in the Italianate style.

Cross Deep in a view looking towards Twickenham with the Pope's Grotto public house on the left, *c.* 1908. The windowless roadside facade of Radnor House is on the right with Cross Deep Hall beyond. All three buildings were destroyed as a result of wartime bombing.

Radnor Gardens in 1907. The Chinese summerhouse dates from the eighteenth century and was originally situated in the riverside gardens of Cross Deep House which stood on the other side of the road and can be glimpsed on the extreme left of the picture.

Radnor Gardens in 1910 in a view looking towards Waldegrave Road. The boys are standing in the channel which cut across the grounds of Cross Deep House, Radnor House and Cross Deep Hall. It was filled in in the 1960s.

Wellesley Road in 1911 with the footbridge of Strawberry Hill Station in the distance. Wentworth House, on the left at the junction with Walpole Gardens, was one of several large houses which have been replaced by modern flats.

Strawberry Hill Station in 1910. The railway line from Twickenham to Teddington had been constructed in 1863 but the station at Strawberry Hill was not opened until 1873. The signal box was demolished in 1977.

Milham's Boat House and Tea Gardens in the early 1900s. Harry Milham established a boatbuilding business on Swan Island, Strawberry Vale, in 1902.

The works of Arthur L. Gibson and Co. which for many years occupied a riverside site in Strawberry Vale. The firm specialized in the manufacture of steel rolling shutters and grilles. The factory moved in 1970, and the site became part of the Mallard Place housing development.

WEST TWICKENHAM

Twickenham Green in a view looking towards the junction of the Staines and Hampton Roads, c. 1912.

Henry Loveland, licensee of the Three Kings public house, *c.* 1900. He died in 1901 whereupon his wife succeeded him as licensee.

The Three Kings public house, *c.* 1900, on its original site in the Heath Road approximately halfway between Copthall Gardens and the junction with King Street. Henry Loveland's name is over the door. The pub was demolished and replaced by the present house in 1913.

Heath Road in a view looking west taken in the 1890s. On the left are the walls and gates of Lismore Lodge, Northumberland House and Savile House, and on the right the walls of Heath House and Laurel Lodge. In the distance is the old Red Lion public house which was replaced by the present building just before the First World War.

Heath Road in a view looking east, with Lion Road to the left in a photograph probably dating from the 1920s. The large houses with extensive grounds to the north of Heath Road have been replaced by shops and the housing in Laurel and Grove Avenues. Savile House, once behind the trees to the right of the picture, was demolished in 1912.

Work on the water main at 'The Dip', Heath Road, 16 May 1902, in a picture taken from the town centre side. Deayton's Stores are on the left, and an advertising hoarding for Frederick Ayland, corn merchant, on the right.

Empire Day on Twickenham Green, *c.* 1910. The celebrations included a march past the flag to music provided by the band from the Metropolitan and City Police Orphanage at Wellesley House in the Hampton Road.

Laying tramlines, Twickenham Green, 19 March 1902. The Green is to the left, and there is a glimpse of Holy Trinity Church to the right. Note the piles of hardwood block paving to the right which was laid between the tracks.

Garden view of Twickenham High School and School of Music, *c*. 1912. The school was founded in 1886 and occupied Nos 61 to 63 The Green. It was run by Miss Harris and Mrs Chapman. The school closed in the early 1930s and Archdeacon Cambridge's Schools now occupy the site.

Laying tramlines in the Hampton Road, 1902. The track, part of the route from Shepherd's Bush to Hampton Court via Isleworth and Twickenham, was constructed by London United Tramways. The service along this section as far as the junction with Stanley Road opened in November 1902 when the fare from Shepherd's Bush was 5*d* (the workmen's rate was 2*d*). The Prince of Wales public house can be seen on the right.

Pupils playing cricket in front of Trafalgar temporary school, *c*. 1905. The iron building was erected in 1904 on the site now occupied by Trafalgar Junior and Infant Schools in Third Cross Road and was in use, accommodating between 150 and 180 children, until late 1906 when the new schools were opened.

Trafalgar School interior group photograph dated 25 September 1912 on the occasion of a presentation to Miss Hill, headmistress of the girls' school, who was leaving to be married in India. The presentation was made by Mr Mears (to the right of the picture) who had been headmaster of the boys' school since it opened in 1904.

Picture of a charabanc outing from Poupart's factory in Third Cross Road taken in the 1920s. William Poupart, a local councillor and churchwarden, had established a market garden in the 1880s at Marsh Farm (extending some 160 acres north of the River Crane to include the sites of the Tertiary College and the Craneford Way council depot), and in 1911 opened the factory in Third Cross Road to make jam from the produce.

Laying tramlines in Stanley Road at the junction with Hampton Road, 18 July 1902. The Nelson public house can just be seen on the right. To the left are the grounds of Wellesley House.

The Metropolitan and City Police Orphanage, Hampton Road, *c.* 1909. The orphanage moved from Fortescue House in the London Road to Hampton Road in 1874, to occupy Wellesley House which had been built in 1852 as Thomas James Scale's Academy and where R.D. Blackmore (author of *Lorna Doone* and later a Teddington resident) taught from 1853 to 1855. The orphanage had accommodation for 200, later increased to 260; the building was subsequently taken over for use as a Shaftesbury Home and was demolished in 1971 to make way for housing development.

Lunchtime in the dining hall of the Metropolitan and City Police Orphanage, *c.* 1906.

The schoolroom of the orphanage, *c.* 1906. The formality and uniformity of the children is very evident from this and the previous picture.

Rear view of the Mall School, Hampton Road. The photograph shows the greenhouse and part of the 3 acres of grounds which originally stretched down to the Stanley Road. The school moved from Teddington to the present site in 1909 and the original Victorian building burnt down in 1960.

Laying tramlines in Stanley Road, 24 July 1902. The row of houses in the background marks the position of South Road. The field to the left is now the site of the fire station.

Clifford's Farm, c. 1913. Also known as Warren or Fulwell Farm, Clifford's Farm stood just north of the River Crane approximately between the present-day Lincoln Avenue and Selkirk Road. Access from the Staines Road was via Mill Road. From the 1880s the farm was owned by John Clifford and later by his son.

Brinsworth House, Staines Road, in a view probably taken soon after the Trustees of the Music Hall Benevolent Institution (now the Entertainment Artistes' Benevolent Fund) purchased Brinsworth House in 1911. The history of the house is uncertain but it is possibly a remodelled early nineteenth-century building. A substantial part of the grounds was disposed of in the Second World War for housing development under the threat of compulsory purchase. The name Brinsworth first appears in 1881 but its origin is unknown.

Staines Road, c. 1919. To the left are the gates and lodge of the Fulwell Park estate which was home to ex-King Manoel of Portugal and his wife Augusta from 1913 until his death in 1932. Fulwell Park, originally Lodge, was built in the early 1600s and demolished and the grounds redeveloped by Wates in the early 1930s. The entrance gates stood approximately halfway between Mill Road and Augusta Road, the latter being one of several street names which retain the royal connection.

WHITTON

*Aerial view across Whitton, May 1931. The old part of Whitton is in the foreground around Prospect
Crescent and Nelson Road. In the centre is the new Redway Estate in process of building. The railway line
runs across the top of the picture.*

A view of Kneller Hall from across the fields, *c.* 1910. This building stands on the site of Sir Godfrey Kneller's house built 1709–11. Kneller's house was demolished in 1847 and the present house constructed. It opened as the Royal Military School of Music in March 1857.

Aerial view of Kneller Hall, 1928. The building on the left is the Duke of Cambridge public house opened in 1857 and at the top left is the old Whitton School.

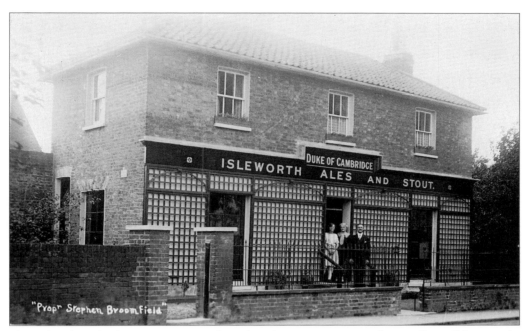

The Duke of Cambridge, *c.* 1930. Opened as a beer house in 1857, just after Kneller Hall became the Royal Military School of Music, it was named after the founder of the music school.

The first Whitton School. It opened its doors in 1851 to provide a practice school for the pupil teachers at Kneller Hall, when it served as a training college. After Nelson School opened in 1928 it became a junior boys' school until it closed in 1960.

The Old Manor House, Whitton Dean, *c.* 1908. The site of a major dwelling since at least 1600, this house was demolished in the 1930s and Old Manor Drive constructed on the site.

Nelson Road, *c.* 1908. The shops on the right were opened in 1907 and the cottages on the left were known as Postman's Rest and Retreat Cottages.

The Old Whitton Post Office, Kneller Road, opposite the White Hart, 1905. Run by the Allenson family from 1846 to 1895, it was later owned by the Vanner family. The house was knocked down in the 1920s and the site became a scrapyard.

Electioneering outside the White Hart in 1906. 'Chinese pigs' refers to 'Chinese slavery', a major issue in the 1906 General Election when Liberal posters portrayed a Chinese coolie. The government had approved a plan to import large numbers of indentured Chinese labourers into the South African Transvaal where they were kept in squalid conditions, although they received a wage. Such exploitation enraged many British men and women and served to sway them against the Tories.

The Old Smithy, Kneller Road, *c.* 1912. This had been a blacksmith's since at least the eighteenth century. It was run by the Stops family from 1910 to 1922 and in the 1920s was converted into a garage, which it remains.

St Philip's and St James's Church, Whitton, *c.* 1910. Consecrated in 1862 it was built on land donated by Maria Gostling of Whitton Park.

Whitton Park House, *c.* 1908. Originally built as a greenhouse by the Duke of Argyll, it was converted into a mansion by the Gostling family who lived there until 1892. The estate was then sold for development and this house was demolished in 1911.

The Tower, Whitton Woods, *c.* 1908. Built by the Duke of Argyll in the 1730s, from it the duke could show his guests a fine panoramic view across Hounslow Heath. The Tower, with Whitton Park House, was demolished in 1911.

William Anderson at the door of his baker's and confectioner's shop, Holly Bush Corner, *c.* 1905. The Anderson family had run this shop as a baker's since 1846. In the 1930s Robert Anderson, who had taken over the business, ran it as a confectioner's until he retired in 1972. The premises then came into use as an Indian restaurant.

The old Nelson public house, decorated for the coronation of George V in 1911. It was opened as a beer house in about 1830 and by 1860 it was a public house. This building was demolished in the 1930s and a new house erected.

View from the Nelson looking towards Kneller Hall, 1905. To the left is the beginning of Hounslow Road, with Anderson's bakery shop and the holly bush which gives Holly Bush Corner its name.

Whitton High Street in 1938. Construction started on shops in Percy Road, Whitton in 1931, and between then and 1939 nearly one hundred shops were opened. Percy Road between the Nelson and the railway bridge was renamed High Street, Whitton in 1937.

Whitton High Street, 1960. In the foreground Mr Raggett is talking to a customer outside his greengrocer's shop, which occupied one of the last remaining cottages in the High Street. The cottages were demolished in 1963 and shops built on the site. Mr Raggett's shop is now the site of the Iceland Freezer Centre.

SECTION SIX

TEDDINGTON

A street scene, c. 1910. It shows tram no. 25 about to pass the Britannia public house, renamed the Hogarth in the 1970s. A horse and cart has passed the wall of St Peter and St Paul's Church on the right-hand side and an obliging onlooker is staring at the camera.

The Causeway, brightly decorated for Christmas, 1907. The newsagent's, W. Bibby, in the foreground, continued to trade until 1944 when, while under the ownership of the father of one of the authors, it sustained bomb damage and was demolished as a dangerous structure. The site was redeveloped in the 1950s and again in 1979 when the whole block was rebuilt.

An unusual view of The Causeway showing the road and pavement flooded and, judging by the heavy cape of the gentleman wading through the water, heavy rain still falling. Although untitled and undated, this is probably one of a series of photographs capturing the freak storm of 14 June 1914. The immediate area had a history of flooding as many underground streams used to drain into the old village pond which was in the middle of the railway track under the bridge.

The Causeway from the Broad Street end. At the far end is the Clarence Hotel and in front of this, on the right, may be seen the scaffolding erected for the building of the town hall which would date the picture to 1883. Another version of this picture is captioned 'Wolsey Road'. This name was an attempt by the Local Board to upgrade the area and exploit the Hampton Court connection. However, the will of the residents finally prevailed and the name reverted to The Causeway.

The Causeway in 1911 decorated with bunting and flags to celebrate the coronation of King George V. The shops seem to be closed and the children appear to be in their Sunday best. The church of St Peter and St Paul is clearly visible in the background.

Flooding in the Broad Street, outside Deayton's Stores. The new sign shows that the premises were in the process of becoming Williamsons, a changeover which took place in 1914. The site became Tesco's in 1956, then Bejams and is now owned by Iceland. The flooding was probably a result of the Great Storm of 14 June 1914.

Broad Street, in a view looking towards the bridge, c. 1905. The tramlines can be clearly seen but the need for traffic lights has not yet arisen. On the left is the wall of Teddington Public School, built by public subscription under the patronage of Queen Adelaide. It opened on 31 January 1832 and was demolished in 1978. On the right is the Provincial Bank which later became Barclays Bank.

Teddington Dairy on the High Street at the corner with Vicarage Road, *c.* 1910. This building was put up through the efforts of two sisters, Louisa and Sally Barber who married two cowherds – Mr Roberts and Mr Prewett. The sisters set about regularizing the milk side of the business and created the dairy. When Mr Roberts died, his widow married Mr Job and the dairy became Job's Dairy. This continued to serve Teddington until the dairy moved to larger premises in Hanworth. The building remained in retail use and survived a mysterious gas explosion in 1981. It was finally demolished when the block was redeveloped in 1991.

Further down the High Street was Poupart's, seen here in about 1920. This was an established business in Hampton and Twickenham making jam. They took over this shop which was previously Marsh Farm Dairy at about the same time as they acquired some of Blackmore's land. The shop became Yogi's Florists in 1990 and on stripping the plywood and hardboard panelling the old dairy tiles and the Marsh Farm name plaque have been discovered and are once more on display.

Milestone & Collis, *c.* 1910. This well-known firm of estate agents was established in 1890. The picture illustrates a very good example of how a shop front was built on to an existing house, in this case the old vicarage, which happened after the coming of the railway. Over 100 years later, the business is still flourishing.

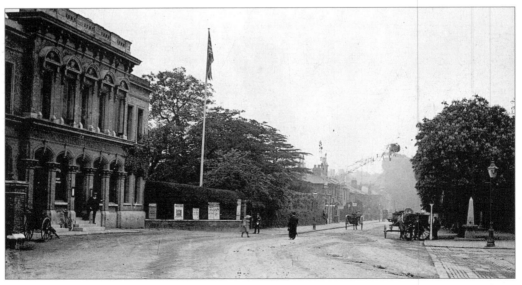

Park Road is one of the oldest thoroughfares in Teddington, and leads to Bushy Park and Hampton. On the left here, in about 1895, is the Clarence Hotel, named to mark the time when the Duke of Clarence was Ranger of Bushy Park. A public house has stood on this site since 1726 called variously the Greyhound, the North Arms, the Guilford Arms and the Clarence Arms. On the opposite side Queen Victoria's Jubilee Drinking Fountain stands in front of Teddington House which was demolished in the late 1950s to make way for the new police station.

A tram passing over Teddington Bridge. The first tram came to Teddington on 2 April 1903, so this picture must have been taken after that date. The bridge is a man-made mound constructed in 1863 to carry vehicular traffic over the railway track. It stands on the site of the old pond which was drained for the railway and it roughly divides the town's old and new parts. The bridge took over two years to build during which period the town was literally divided with traffic having to travel to Hampton Wick or Strawberry Hill to cross the line.

A traffic-free High Street, c. 1903. The recently completed Grand Parade occupies the centre of the picture and the tramlines and rails are plainly visible. The premises of Lemon's Bakery stand on the right. Apart from providing daily bread, Lemon's were high-class confectioners and caterers. The Lemons were a long-established and influential Teddington family whose members were active in all walks of life.

The snow-covered High Street seen from the Langham Road end. This is probably one of a series of photographs taken on Boxing Day 1906 when Teddington Weir was frozen over. Such scenes were popular to send to soldiers fighting the Dutch in South Africa. On the extreme left is Faversham House, which was demolished in 1918. Further down is the Royal Oak public house, which at that time extended on to the pavement.

St Alban's Fête at Chesfield. Chesfield was one of several old houses of Hampton Wick on the Lower Teddington Road and was the venue for the St Alban's Fête on 22 June 1907, held to raise money for the completion of the church. The vicar, Revd Francis Leith Boyd, is third from the right in the front row and the Mayor of Kingston, decked in his chain of office, stands roughly in the centre.

St Alban's Church, possibly the most controversial church ever constructed in Teddington, in a picture taken in 1905. It was the idea of Revd Francis Leith Boyd and was designed by local architect William Niven. However, a church on this scale did not find favour with all parishioners; R.D. Blackmore spoke out against it and refused to pledge his support. Nevertheless, an extensive fund-raising campaign enabled the building work to commence in 1885 with the foundation stone being laid by the Bishop of London, Dr Temple, on 29 April 1887. The building was consecrated, unfinished, in 1889 and served as the parish church until 1967 when dwindling congregations caused it to be made redundant.

St Alban's Festival, 21 June 1908. Originally due to have been held on Wednesday 17 June, the proposed procession was disrupted by the Kensitites. These were members of the Kensit Wickliffe Preachers' Mission, a hard-line puritanical movement. They followed the Bible implicitly and objected to the 'Popery' of the High Church; they disrupted several church processions. This picture shows the rearranged event held on Sunday 21 June. Although not obvious from this picture, there was a heavy police presence: the crossbearer and acolytes were accompanied by ten policemen on foot and others on horseback. The Kensit party took up their position on the corner of Kingston Lane but were moved on by the mounted police. Both parties came face to face at the triangle opposite Elmfield House with the cheering and hissing of the crowd drowning the music of the Ham and Petersham Brass Band. The procession passed without incident and returned to St Alban's for the morning service.

St Alban's Church interior. Having had the church built, the Revd Boyd then had the problem of furnishing it in an appropriate style. Fortunately the parishioners came to the rescue and this photograph shows some of the items donated: the pulpit was a gift of Mr John Pullman, designed by Mr A.H. Skipworth and constructed by Mr L.A. Turner; the altar ornaments were made in Florence to a classic design and presented by Mrs Scott; the altar frontals were presented by Mrs Chinnery and Miss Sweete and the marble floor by Henry Chinnery.

Teddington Cottage Hospital. In 1874 a public meeting determined that Teddington would have its own hospital and on 20 March 1875 the Teddington and Hampton Wick Cottage Hospital opened in Elfin Villas, Elfin Grove (so called after their architect, Laurence Finn). The hospital survived many early crises, some financial, and an extension and a dispensary were added. With the local population continuing to grow, the facilities were proving inadequate and at the end of the First World War a fresh bout of fund-raising commenced in aid of the combined project of a war memorial and a new hospital.

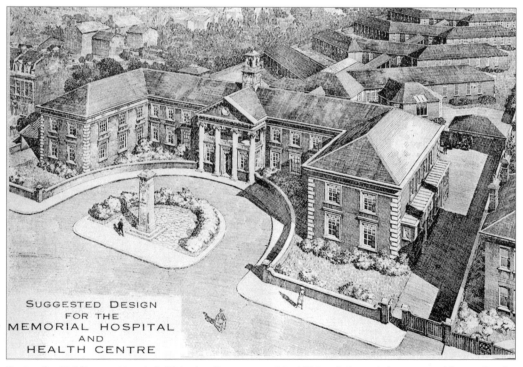

Design for Teddington Hospital. This plan first appeared in 1924 and showed the proposed layout for the new Teddington Memorial Hospital and Health Centre incorporating the war memorial to the fallen of the First World War. The present hospital building is fairly similar.

English's Bakery, Stanley Road, complete with delivery van parked outside in a picture taken in the 1930s. Local directories list Peter English as a baker here for many years. The shop on the right is Bray & Co., chemists. Some sixty years later, it is interesting that the same trades are carried on on these premises with Belmonts Bakery and D. Thomas the chemist.

John Frederick Latham outside his draper's shop at No. 2 Hughendon Terrace, Stanley Road, Upper Teddington. Posted on 23 December 1907, this card conveyed Christmas greetings to a friend in Southsea. John Latham ran the business from 1898 to 1922 when it was taken over by Albert Edward Garrud still as a draper's. When the Post Office renumbered the road, the shop became No. 160 Stanley Road and has remained a retail shop until the present time. The holes in the facia where the gas lamps hung can still be seen. A greengrocer's has just closed on the site.

Coburg Road was laid out in about 1863 but no houses were built at that time. By 1893, however, the Ordnance Survey map shows that a few houses had been constructed on the south side and more were built between Anlaby and King's Roads. At this time there were still nurseries on both sides. The majority of housing was erected between 1894 and 1914 and with the coming of the First World War, the name was changed to Connaught Road on a wave of anti-German feeling.

The Horse and Groom public house in Waldegrave Road was built in the 1880s. The advertising board proclaims: 'The Horse and Groom/Livery and Bait Stables/Teddington/Proprietor: W. Strugnell.' On the left-hand side is Waldegrave Avenue, possibly the smallest road in Teddington with only six houses. In 1937, the proprietor is described as a beer retailer which suggests that the business only held a beer licence. The pub closed for the last time on 19 April 1996 and is to become a Pizza Express restaurant. This early photograph probably dates from the 1890s.

The Willoughby Hotel on the corner of Church and Argyle Roads, *c.* 1910. Built in the 1890s, it appears to have been more of a public house than a hotel. During the Second World War the building was probably the site of the worst single disaster to befall Teddington when on 29 November 1940 it was totally destroyed by bombing with a loss of seventeen lives.

Church Lane is a small road running off Church Road and parallel to it back to the road bridge. This scene shows the road and certainly all of its younger occupants who are surveying the mess in the aftermath of the exceptionally heavy rainstorm of 14 June 1914.

Teddington Trades Exhibition, 1908. The second of these exhibitions was held in a field in Station Road – described in the local paper as Teddington's White City – between 22 and 26 September. A huge marquee opened by Dr Coalbank housed a number of stalls representing the business life of Teddington. Ten thousand visitors came to the exhibition and the organizers decided to keep it open for a further day so enabling an additional one thousand two hundred people to attend. This picture shows the stand of the Hampton Court Gas Co. who had their offices at Bridge Approach, Hampton Wick. The last of their gasometers was demolished in 1993.

Teddington Fire Brigade, c. 1900. Teddington used to have its own volunteer fire brigade. In 1831, they purchased their own fire engine which was housed at the public school and later moved to Park Lane. This picture is displayed at the fire station next to the library on Waldegrave Road. Captain of the brigade was Algernon Frampton who was responsible for developing a policy of cooperation with the other local brigades. The houses opposite the fire station were owned by the local authority and were used to accommodate firemen and their families. The Teddington brigade continued in service until 26 July 1938 when it amalgamated with Twickenham. Its Chief Officer, Stephen Russell, was then appointed Deputy Chief Fire Officer for the Borough of Twickenham.

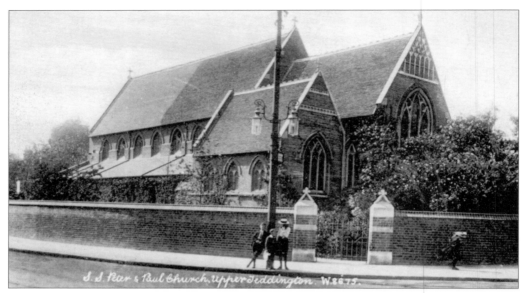

St Peter and St Paul's Church, Broad Street, *c.* 1905. The church was built as a chapel of ease to St Mary's by Revd Daniel Trinder in 1865 to cope with the increasing population which resulted from the railway's coming to Teddington. The area became a separate parish in 1880 but was reduced in size when the further parish of St Michael and St George was created in Fulwell in 1914. The building shown here was demolished between December 1978 and January 1979 and a new church, dedicated in September 1980, was built opposite on the site of the old public school.

Broad Street, from the Hampton end, *c.* 1905. The tram is turning into Stanley Road, heading towards Fulwell Depot. Goulds the chemist's is on the left-hand side and later moved down Broad Street into premises on the opposite side. The original site was redeveloped in 1991. Honey's the grocer's store sustained some bomb damage in 1944 and was eventually pulled down to make way for road widening. The Queen public house closed its doors in the 1950s and the site is now occupied by a betting shop and launderette.

The Old Church, Teddington. St Mary's had always been the parish church ever since Benedictine monks established a chapel on the site before the Norman Conquest. There have been many colourful priests here over the centuries, perhaps none more so than the Revd Dr Stephen Hales, parish priest from 1709 to 1761. During this period he virtually rebuilt the church, financing much of the work personally. Relieved of its parish duties when St Alban's was consecrated in 1885, St Mary's continued as a chapel of ease until 1967 when the parish was renamed St Mary with St Alban and St Mary's once again became the parish church.

St Mary's Church interior. This photograph shows the old stained glass which, sadly, was destroyed in July 1944 when a flying bomb landed in the area. The glass was replaced by the present windows in 1960.

Garden party at Rutherford on a postcard dated 7 April 1909. Rutherford was one of the larger old houses in Queen's Road at the Park Road end. On the back has been written: 'Do you see me in the corner with my hands behind me? A garden party here last Whitsuntide. K.'

The Wesleyan Chapel at the junction of Stanley and Hampton Roads, *c.* 1910. Built in 1879 to accommodate the congregation that had outgrown the chapel at Craig Hall, it was destroyed by a flying bomb in 1944. When the present Methodist church was built on the site, the actual building was set further back from the road to leave a green in front to complement the war memorial by the hospital.

Fred M. Millis in a punt at the rear of his house Wattle Bloom in Broom Water where he resided from 1904 to 1905. He seems to have been connected with the world of entertainment and gave his telegraphic address as 'Voices Teddington'. Several personalized cards like this have been discovered, having been posted internally in Australia.

Trowlock Island. A small island off the Middlesex bank of the Thames near the Lensbury Club, it is connected to the mainland by a chain ferry and houses the headquarters of the Royal Canoe Club. Trowlock Island takes its name from a type of Thames barge – a trow – which is used to carry loads of between 50 and 60 tons. The island was also the headquarters of Harry Gibbs's boatbuilding business which was set up in 1910 and continued until 1940. Today the island is occupied by several chalet-style bungalows.

Teddington Bridge. This view is of the second section of the bridge going from Lock Island across the Lock Cut to the Surrey Bank. Completely different from the main suspension bridge, this is a fixed section and was originally part of Hammersmith Bridge. This section has a span of 99 feet and connects to the ground by an 18 feet flight of steps.

Teddington Suspension Bridge, c. 1930. In 1882 Henry Taunt had written, 'A bridge is sadly needed as the watermen here demand the extortionate sum of threepence as their fee from passengers crossing the ferry.' Many must have agreed for this bridge replaced the old ferry service and was constructed in 1889 at a cost of £2,700. It was built in two sections, the main one, shown here, spanning the river from the Anglers to the Lock Island. It is a lasting monument to the local board who commissioned George Pooley to design it. This section is a suspension bridge of 160 feet with a 6 feet width and was constructed by Messrs Goddard and Massey of Nottingham.

The Weir, Teddington. A fish weir was established here in the Middle Ages and bills for its repair in 1537 have been found in the Muniment Room of Westminster Abbey. The present weir was built in 1812 and was a simple overfall across the river to the Lock Island with a central section controlled by paddles. Major upgrading was carried out in 1871 and 1897. In 1940 enemy bombing damaged the weir and a disused barge was used to patch the breach until long after hostilities had ceased. A full rebuilding programme was completed in 1994.

A view of the main lock at Teddington with a full passenger steamer passing through, c. 1900. On the shore many people, dressed in their Sunday best, have gathered to watch the progress of the boats through the locks. This picture epitomizes the Victorians' love of boating and the river. The years between 1880 and 1900 saw the 'Golden Age' of boating and the Victorians flocked on to the river in every kind of boat imaginable.

The Lock, Teddington. The first lock at Teddington was a timber construction built by the City of London Corporation and opened on 20 June 1811. The lock was rebuilt in the 1850s when a sidelock for pleasure craft was added. A brass plaque noting the laying of the foundation stone on 3 June 1857 was discovered in 1950 during renovation work. A boatslide was added to the sidelock and this may be seen in front of the bridge.

Teddington Locks, c. 1905. This picture shows the first lock on the left-hand side and the larger double or barge lock on the right. It was opened on 11 June 1904 by the local MP, Sir Frederick D. Dixon-Hartland.

HAMPTON WICK

Ancient and modern at Hampton Court, c. 1910. This picture could be entitled 'Transport in the Park' as it shows just about every form of road transport of the time. A horse-drawn coach is entering the park followed by a motor bus; on the left-hand side a convertible motor car is about to leave followed by a motorcycle. There are bicycles on the bank in the foreground.

Glamorgan Road, Hampton Wick, *c.* 1910. One of the tree-lined roads in Hampton Wick, it runs from Seymour Road to Normansfield Avenue. A comparison drawn today would clearly highlight the absence of motor cars from this scene; the road is now filled with traffic.

Old Cottages, Park Road, Hampton Wick, in a picture taken by Teddington photographers Young & Co., *c.* 1910. Built around 1700, these cottages represent one of the oldest surviving parts of Hampton Wick.

The baker's shop of Robert John Belchamber on the High Street, Hampton Wick, *c.* 1910. Belchamber was born in 1858 and educated at the Endowed School. After serving his apprenticeship he joined the family bakery business, taking over in 1889. He was a larger-than-life character, serving as a councillor on the Local Board for over thirty years and as Fire Superintendent of Hampton Wick Fire Station. He was also an active member of the football, cricket, rugby and hockey clubs. He died in 1948 and the *Surrey Comet* described his funeral as 'The Funeral of the King of Hampton Wick'.

High Street, Hampton Wick, 1902. This view shows the old Swan on the right and the Forresters with the Jubilee Drinking Fountain in front of it on the left. The present day Swan was built after the High Street was widened in 1902 to take trams.

High Street, Hampton Wick, c. 1895. Another view taken before the road was widened. On the left is the White Hart public house when the building was standing flush to the road. The buildings on the right were demolished in 1902.

A tram coming over Kingston Bridge into Hampton Wick, *c.* 1910. This bridge was built in 1828 and was a toll bridge until 1870. The first tram went over on 2 April 1903; a test-run had taken place at night on 23 March. It was not until 1 March 1906 that the inaugural ceremony was performed by the Mayor of Kingston, who drove a tram from Hampton Wick to the top of Kingston Hill, and the service then commenced. After many years of wear, the bridge is currently being strengthened.

Upper Teddington Road, *c.* 1910. This road is an extension of Hampton Wick High Street, joining the Kingston Road at Teddington. The picture shows a Kingston-bound tram that has just passed Normansfield Hospital.

Lower Teddington Road, *c.* 1910. This road runs from the Swan public house at Hampton Wick to become Broom Road at the border with Teddington. The picture has been taken towards Teddington, a little way past Wolsey's Cottage.

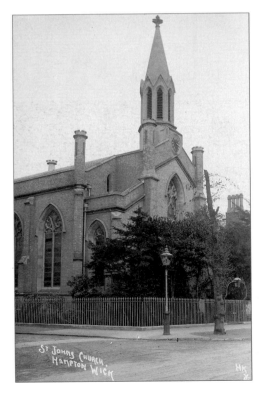

St John's Church, *c.* 1910. The Church of St John the Baptist was built in 1831 and became a parish church in its own right in 1834. Designed by a local architect, Edward Lapidge of Lower Teddington Road, it has undergone many alterations in its time but is now in a poor state of repair. With a dwindling congregation and ever increasing costs, it is likely to be declared redundant in the near future.

A group of women and children skating on one of the ponds in Home Park. The scene is a reminder of a once regular winter sport. The picture is undated but is probably of the winter of 1906/7 when the Thames froze over at Kingston and a horse and cart were driven across it. Skating was a popular winter pastime and it is surprising to see how many people had their own skates.

A more common view of the Home Park pond, taken in early summer, *c.* 1930.

Interior of St John's Church, *c.* 1920. The photograph shows the stained glass (above the altar) depicting the Ascension. This was donated by parishioners in memory of Revd De Crispigny in 1888.

Suffolk House. This is a fine example of a typical Hampton Wick villa built about 1850. The house still stands in Church Grove; the porch has been removed, the upper windows replaced by larger modern dormer windows and the front wall and railings are gone. The tree, looking a little more gnarled and knotted, is still in the same position.

Home Park gates, *c.* 1910. The gates marked the main entrance to Home Park with the Old King's (Henry VII) Head public house on the right. This picture shows the rebuilt pub of 1906.

Hampton Wick Station. Opened in 1863, the station was the last on the Kingston loop of the London and South Western Line. In 1888 this was the scene of a serious crash when a light engine collided with a passenger train. Three passengers were killed and fifteen injured. The station was rebuilt in 1969 with its present-day rather characterless facade.

The Vicarage, Hampton Wick. This was the first vicarage in the village. It was given by the Lord Chancellor in 1855 and stood opposite the Cobblers Walk Gate to Bushy Park. In some photographs it is called 'The Parsonage'. It is now the site of Ingram House.

Normansfield, Hampton Wick, *c.* 1920. Built in 1856 and originally called the White House, the building was acquired, unfinished, in 1858 by Dr John Langdon-Down as his home and as a hospital for his mentally handicapped patients. During his life here he pioneered work on the identification and treatment of Down's Syndrome, which bears his name. The house ceased to be privately owned in 1951 when it came into the possession of the National Health Service. The current 'Care in the Community' programme means that the hospital is no longer needed and it is due to close in 1997. Plans have been submitted to turn it into a conference centre.

Home Park Tea Gardens. After Bushy and Home Parks were opened to the public, they quickly became popular weekend attractions for Londoners. Several establishments such as this one sprang up to cater for the crowds.

Hampton Wick and Kingston Bridge. This aerial view shows the main road over Kingston Bridge forking to the left towards Hampton Court and to the right into Hampton Wick village.

The Willow Camp Tea Gardens. This unusual picture shows a refreshments garden on the bank of the river. The garden is probably on the site of what has become the Aries Sailing Club which is owned by the BBC Sports Club. The distinctive corrugated-iron hut on the right survived until the early 1980s.

Thirlmere, Hampton Wick. A typical postcard of a family outside their home in Hampton Wick, this was sent to friends in Richmond, wishing them a Happy Christmas in 1905. It is a good example of how the early postcards were used; in this case as a greetings card.

BUSHY PARK

Bushy Park, c. 1910. Although famous for its avenue of horse chestnut trees, Bushy Park also contains many other species. This mighty oak was probably planted to mark the boundary between Hampton and Teddington parishes.

Skating in Bushy Park. This card was sent to a soldier at York Barracks on 2 February 1907. The sender had been present on the previous Sunday when the photograph was taken but she did not say if she was in it. The winter of 1906/7 was particularly cold.

The King's Canadian Convalescent Hospital. In 1913 the buildings of Upper Lodge in Bushy Park became vacant. On the commencement of the First World War, which broke out shortly afterwards, King George V gave permission for Upper Lodge to be used as a hospital for wounded Canadian soldiers. Two of the nurses and several patients are shown here standing in the grounds.

Main entrance to the King's Canadian Convalescent Hospital, *c.* 1915. The hospital continued in use until 1919.

Another view of the hospital showing wounded soldiers relaxing in the grounds. The tower of the theatre can be seen in the background.

The King's Canadian Convalescent Hospital. This picture shows the prefabricated theatre that was built here for the entertainment of the wounded. It is still standing today.

Morning assembly at the King's Canadian School, *c.* 1925. When the hospital closed after the war, King George V granted the use of Upper Lodge to the London County Council as a holiday home for under-privileged boys from East London. It could accommodate up to 290 boys at any one time and all lessons were held in the open.

The King's Canadian School with the daily post being distributed among the boys, *c.* 1925.

A hurricane struck in Teddington on 1 June 1908. The *Thames Valley Times* carried a report of the disaster and after the news had spread, sightseers flocked in droves to the park to view the damage for themselves. This picture, by Young & Co. of Teddington, shows a family outing, probably at the Teddington Gate end. Some of the more adventurous children have climbed the split tree stump and an early pram can be seen in the foreground.

Devastation to Chestnut Avenue in the aftermath of the hurricane of 1 June 1908. The *Thames Valley Times* claimed that sixty-one trees, principally limes, had been uprooted in a matter of minutes. The report stated that the chestnut trees in the avenue were not greatly damaged, 'only a limb here and there having been broken off'. However, this picture, showing many horse chestnut trees down, would suggest otherwise. The building on the left at the end of the avenue is Bushy Park Lodge.

One of the popular pastimes in Bushy Park was watching or taking part in the coaching marathon. Several of these were held here and seemed to run on similar lines to the bicycle meets. This picture dates from *c.* 1909.

Bushy Park Lodge, *c.* 1910. This house was often referred to as Bushy Lodge, and stood roughly where Avenue Gardens joins Park Road today. It was built about 1815 and later became a favourite spot with Queen Mary. In its later period it became a nursing home. The house was demolished in 1925 to make way for Avenue Gardens. The coach-house still survives.

Under Chestnut Avenue, 19 May 1937. Taken at the Lion Gate end, this picture demonstrates the great area of shade afforded by the horse chestnut trees.

Outing to Bushy Park. This untitled card merely carries the caption 'Bushy Park – June 26th 1926'. It was clearly a significant event, with over 150 people in the picture.

This photograph of visitors feeding the deer in Bushy Park was taken from the Hampton Court end of the park. The deer were tamer in the 1920s than they are now!

Diana Pond was dug on the instructions of Sir Christopher Wren in 1713 as part of his plan for the grand entrance to Hampton Court Palace for William and Mary. At the same time the Chestnut Avenue was planted and it was intended that the Great Hall would be rebuilt to become the focal point on entry through the Lion Gates.

Next to the Heron Pond was the Boating Pool where, until the 1970s, a variety of rowing boats, paddle boats and canoes would appear every spring ready for the summer season. It is not clear whether the franchise was not renewed or whether the venture ceased to be profitable, but all trace of the boating activity has now disappeared. Both pictures on this page date from the 1930s.

The Diana Fountain, *c.* 1920. This statue was commissioned by Charles I for his queen, Henrietta Maria. It was called Arethusa and originally stood in the grounds of Somerset House but was later moved to the Privy Gardens at Hampton Court. It was moved by Wren in 1713 to its present site at a cost of £2,000. Over the years the name Arethusa has fallen into disuse and after a short spell as Venus, the statue is now Diana.

The Pavilion restaurant/cafeteria stood next to the children's playground at the Hampton Court end of the park. It is seen here in about 1920, but burnt down in the 1950s and was never rebuilt. Not to rebuild on such a prestigious site implies that it was not trading profitably or perhaps was not insured. No trace of the structure now remains.

The Bird Sanctuary which is in fact part of the Woodland Gardens and possibly the Waterhouse Plantation. These gardens were originally part of the Pheasantry and are very popular as a safe haven and nesting ground for birds and water fowl.

Timothy Bennett, the cordwainer or shoemaker of Hampton Wick who took on the Earl of Halifax over the closure of Bushy Park. In 1734 Halifax was the Ranger of Bushy Park and commenced building a brick wall around its perimeter. When this was completed in 1737, it cut off all the footpaths through the park from Hampton Wick to Hampton. As Hampton Wick was in the parish of Hampton at that time, it meant that all Hampton Wick parishioners were forced to take the long route to church on Sundays by walking around the perimeter wall and then along the river road. Timothy Bennett issued proceedings against Halifax for illegal closure of the park and although Halifax dismissed him as an 'impertinent fellow', he did reconsider and open the gates to the park. The case was dropped and Bennett was praised as a local worthy enjoying general esteem until he died two years later in his seventy-seventh year. The footpath from Hampton Wick to Hampton is now called Cobbler's Walk and a mezzotint memorial to Bennett was unveiled by J.C. Buckmaster in 1900.

HAMPTON

Thames Street in a view looking west taken c. 1905. The old post office, on the extreme left, later moved to High Street and then to Station Road. The sign of the Crown can be seen on the right, a pub which gave up its licence in 1909 and whose landlords can be traced back to 1791. The old fire station, with its arched doorway, can also be seen.

The Karsino, Tagg's Island, opened by Fred Karno in 1913. In 1872 Tom Tagg, who had established a boat-building business on the island in 1868, took over a ramshackle beerhouse, the Angler's Retreat, and built the Island Hotel. Later his son George Tagg took over the business, but custom fell away until Fred Karno took over the lease in 1912.

Boating and other riverside activity at the Karsino, c. 1914. The Karsino was a luxurious and popular complex with many facilities when it opened in 1913. However, its popularity waned after the First World War and various name changes were tried including the Thames Riviera, the Palm Beach and the Casino. In 1940 A.C. Cars moved to the island and the first bridge was built. This was replaced by the present bridge in 1982.

Interior of St Albans, *c.* 1920. This was a large riverside dwelling formerly in Hampton Court Road; the oldest part of the house dated from 1692. It was occupied by Robert Graham (who founded the Volunteer Fire Brigade) from around 1875. His daughter, the novelist Winifred Graham and her husband Theodore Cory bequeathed the house to the Borough of Twickenham in 1961. It became unsafe and was demolished in 1972.

A view of Hampton Regatta in 1923. There were a number of regattas held on the stretch of river between Hampton and Molesey. The oldest event was the Watermen's Regatta first run in 1835 and held annually thereafter until 1910. During this period it was also called the Watermen's and Fishermen's Regatta and, from 1895, the Tradesmen's and Watermen's Regatta. The Hampton Regatta was a descendant of the Watermen's Regatta.

A view of the river towards Garrick's Temple and St Mary's Church, *c.* 1925. The building attached to Garrick's Temple is Temple House. The house only existed from 1923 to 1932 for there was such strong feeling against having the building attached to the temple that it was bought by the council and demolished. Garrick's Lawn then became the recreation ground which still contains Garrick's Temple to Shakespeare.

Fête beside Garrick's Temple, 9 July 1908. The temple has been illuminated and a brass band is playing in what was then part of the grounds of the Garrick Villa estate. The temple was built by David Garrick in 1755 as a monument to Shakespeare. Roubillac sculpted a statue of the Bard to stand in a niche in the temple; this is now in the British Museum.

David Garrick, the great actor, moved to Hampton House (now Garrick's Villa) in 1754. He died in 1779 but his widow Eva lived there until her death in 1822 (at the age of ninety-eight). Numerous alterations were made to the house by Robert Adam during Garrick's tenure. The portico and its arched podium are made of wood and date from around 1756. This photograph dates from *c.* 1915.

Four decorated trams outside Garrick's Villa, *c.* 1907. Sir Clifton Robinson, managing director of London United Tramways, lived in Garrick's Villa when this picture was taken. LUT had acquired the property when the road was widened for double tram tracks and Garrick's Villa lost 20 feet from its frontage. Treats were held for employees and their families in the grounds, as depicted here.

The old Feathers, built *c.* 1540. This building is the oldest in Hampton and was formerly the Feathers Inn. Originally a church house, it was rented out as an inn from the early seventeenth century until it ceased trading as an inn in 1792. It was subsequently divided into cottages, the middle one of which is still called Feather's Cottage.

Delivery boy for Miles the Baker's in Station Road, Hampton, *c.* 1903. The picture was taken in Thames Street (outside the churchyard and vicarage garden walls) which still looks very similar today, some ninety years later. Note the muddy condition of the road which fortunately has changed – but the present volume of traffic would never allow a stationary vehicle to pose for a photograph!

The old St Mary's Church, demolished in 1829. The new church, constructed on the same site, opened in 1831. It is not known when the old church was built, although there have been vicars of Hampton since at least 1342. The old church was a much altered building of medieval origin with a large schoolroom on the north side of the chancel and various other additions.

The new St Mary's Church, c. 1905. The old church had contained many fine monuments, many of which are preserved in the new church. The new building can accommodate approximately twice as many people as the old one. In 1884 new pews were installed, replacing the old box-type pews and in 1887 the chancel was added to commemorate Queen Victoria's Golden Jubilee. A number of stained-glass windows have since been donated by various benefactors.

Testing out the hoses of a new fire engine in 1924. This picture of the riverside in Bell Hill Recreation Ground shows part of the celebrations in connection with the arrival of a new fire engine named after Alice Graham, widow of Robert Graham, founder of the Volunteer Fire Brigade in 1885 and who was associated with it until his death in 1922.

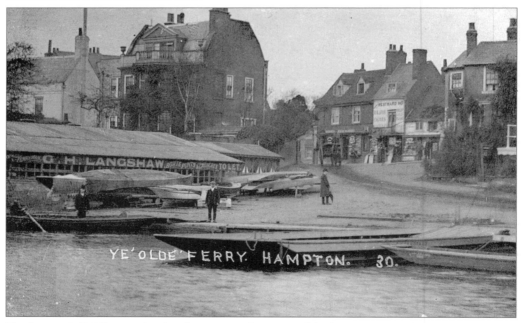

The ferry at Bell Hill, near the church, c. 1905. This is one of the longest running ferries in the country, operating since at least 1519. At the time this picture was taken the ferry was the large flat-bottomed boat which was extremely popular on Hurst Park racedays. Nowadays the ferry is a smaller boat. The building on the extreme right is the old Ferry House, demolished in 1914.

The Bell Hotel, *c.* 1930. This picture is of an unspecified occasion with a coach and horses drawn up outside the Bell. The Bell was rebuilt in 1893 after a fire in 1892 had destroyed the old building. The proceeds from the lease of the earlier premises had been bequeathed in 1557, by Robert Hammond, to establish a Free School. This school was the forerunner of Hampton School.

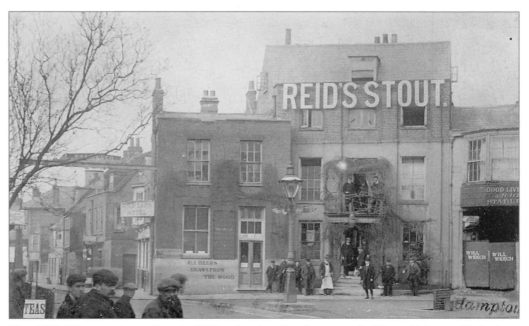

The old Red Lion was burnt down in 1908 and replaced by the present building which stayed in business until about 1980 when it was converted into offices. The old Red Lion was known as the Shipp until the 1750s, and parts of it were very old, possibly of Tudor origin. It is known that the Lawrence family were landlords for upwards of 100 years, from *c.* 1770 to *c.* 1875.

The new Red Lion, *c.* 1934. The pub, then under new proprietorship, had been built in 1909 to replace the earlier building which was burnt down. In order to widen Thames Street, the old Red Lion had to be rebuilt, and Captain Graham of the Volunteer Fire Brigade obtained permission to set fire to the building to provide practice for the brigade.

View of High Street, *c.* 1903. The large building on the left-hand side, with the pantile roof, was replaced shortly afterwards by the present building which was occupied by Barclays Bank for many years. The sign for the Jolly Gardeners can be seen; it stayed in business until the 1950s when it became Heath's the boatbuilders. The buildings on the right are virtually unchanged today, some ninety years on.

A butcher's shop in High Street. At the time this photograph was taken the premises were occupied by Messrs Farmer and later by Stacey's the butcher's, who traded for many decades up to the 1980s. The tricycle in the foreground must have been one of the earliest bicycle-based delivery vehicles ever designed. The premises were occupied by butchers for over a century. The yard is now used for the repair of Morris Minor cars.

Thames Street in a view looking east towards St Mary's Church, c. 1860. The sign for the Red Lion hanging across the street bears the name Lawrence — the family who were landlords for over a century, until around 1875. Some old and interesting shop fronts can be seen on the left-hand side of the road. Thames Street was the main shopping street at this time, before the advent of the motor car.

The old fire station in Thames Street, *c.* 1918. The brigade had been formed in 1885 under the captaincy of Robert Graham who lived in the large riverside house, St Albans, which was demolished in 1972. The three foundation stones of the fire station were laid by Captain Graham in 1897 and it opened for service in February 1898. An enormous influence on the brigade, Graham was associated with it until his death in 1922.

Hampton Volunteer Fire Brigade outing, *c.* 1910. This picture of a day trip shows the firemen on Bournemouth pier. There was great camaraderie among the members, and great competition to get into the Volunteer Fire Brigade. Many social events took place at Graham's home, St Albans, in Hampton Court Road, including billiards evenings and dinners.

A Metropolitan Water Board fire brigade's Merryweather Escape, *c.* 1905. This splendid early Escape dates from *c.* 1905. The water board had their own separate fire brigade, often better equipped than the Hampton volunteer brigade. The water board brigade was commanded by Sir John Restler, general manager of the waterworks. The two brigades often competed to reach a fire first.

The steam engine *Sunbury* on the Metropolitan Water Board Light Railway, *c.* 1920. This narrow gauge (2 feet) railway was constructed in 1915 to transport coal from the riverside coal wharf to the coal-fired waterworks pumping stations in Hampton and Kempton Park. Three engines were used on this railway named *Hampton, Kempton* and *Sunbury* and the line continued in use until around the time of the Second World War.

The Upper Sunbury Road, *c.* 1905. Formerly the Staines Road, this was one of the three ancient thoroughfares that dictated the modern road plan of Hampton. The other two roads were the Lower Sunbury Road (previously the Chertsey Road) and the Twickenham (or Heath) Road, now known as the High Street. The muddy road surface is an interesting comparison with the busy tarmacked road of today.

Hampton Grammar School, Upper Sunbury Road, *c.* 1925. The school was originally founded in 1557 and in 1726 a new schoolroom was built on the north side of the chancel of St Mary's Church, but this was lost when the old church was demolished in 1829. Five years later a new school was built on the site of the present parish hall. In 1880 the school moved to a new building in Upper Sunbury Road where it remained until 1939 when it transferred to Hanworth Road.

St Mary's (Cottage) Hospital, in Upper Sunbury Road, *c.* 1914. Built in 1912/13, the hospital was founded by an endowment from a wealthy resident, Mr T. Foster-Knowles, on land adjoining the old grammar school, and was used as a military hospital in the First World War. During the 1980s and '90s the hospital's services were gradually cut back and, despite massive community fund-raising efforts and support, the hospital was closed in 1994.

Priory Road, *c.* 1925, before it was made up. It is a very old road marking the northern boundary of the large Old Field. Oldfield Road follows the western and southern boundaries of the ancient field, and part of the Tudor Road completes the eastern boundary. On Rocque's map of 1754 Priory Road is shown as Clea (later Clay) Lane.

Priory Road Post Office and shops, *c.* 1905. This view is one of a small series of postcards issued by this post office just after the turn of the century. Some ninety years later the view is little changed. The post office is still on the same site and the shops, although in different hands, look much the same. The lack of traffic is the obvious clue to the date of this picture!

Coronation Parade, Station Road, 1937. This view, looking up Station Road from the junction with High Street, shows part of the festivities held to celebrate the coronation of George VI and Queen Elizabeth (now the Queen Mother). The houses on the left date from around 1880 and have since been replaced by Algar Court.

The police station in Station Road decorated for the coronation of George V on 22 June 1911. The station, now used by the metropolitan police's traffic division, was built in 1905. The old police station had been located at No. 12 Station Road in premises now used for commercial purposes.

Aerial view of the Grand Junction Reservoir and the south-western corner of Hampton, *c.* 1929. Left of centre is the cottage hospital and centre right the old grammar school. Bloxham Crescent can be seen clearly top left. Numerous nurseries and glasshouses – the long white buildings – are visible top left; these were later built over.

Percy Road School (now Hampton Junior School) when newly built in 1907. Previously the school had shared premises with Hampton Grammar School in a building on the site of the present parish hall. The English (lower) school continued to grow after the Latin (upper) school moved to Upper Sunbury Road in 1880. The new lower school was completed in 1907.

The railway station and old bridge at Hampton Station, *c.* 1905. The railway first arrived in 1864, when it was only single track, and the station building on the right dates from that time. Double tracks were opened in 1878 and the old footbridge was opened in 1894. The new station buildings were built in 1897. The old footbridge was replaced by the present concrete one in the 1930s.

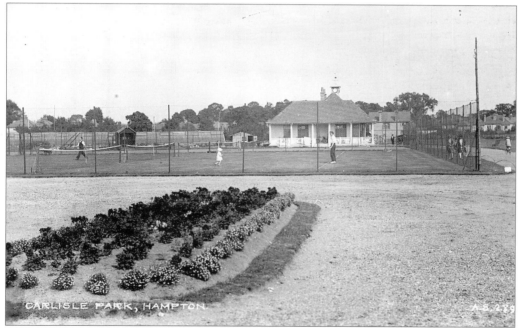

Carlisle Park Recreation Ground in the 1930s. The park is named after the 9th Earl of Carlisle who was the owner of the Manor Park estate, of which the park was part. The estate was developed for housing from 1897 onwards. This process took several decades and the Manor House was not demolished until 1935/6 after which the land surrounding it was developed.

Hampton Swimming Pool in a photograph believed to have been taken on opening day in 1922. It was closed in 1980 to save money but a campaign was started by local residents to preserve the pool. Their action resulted in the pool being transferred to the Hampton Pool Group and, with funds raised from the community and grants, the now heated pool was re-opened in 1985.

The Manor House, demolished in 1935–6, stood on the site of the present Manor Gardens, the last part of the Manor House estate to be developed. The building dated from the eighteenth century and replaced an earlier seventeenth-century house. Near the Manor House was the Manor House Farm as well as several large ponds, including those known as Townsend Ponds, and an old ice-house.

Uxbridge Road near the junction with High Street, *c.* 1940. This view shows the newly built houses in Howard Close which runs beside the Uxbridge Road. This section of the former Manor House estate was among the last to be developed, following the demolition of the Manor House and the sale of the last remnants of the estate in 1935–6.

The Uxbridge Road, formerly the Hounslow Road, at the junction with Hanworth Road, *c.* 1905. In 1895 it was asphalted from the junction with High Street to the Windmill Bridge. The local board, which was only formed in 1890, became an urban district council in 1895 and the new body was obviously keen to get on and improve the roads.

A delivery cart loaded with crates marked 'Hampton' from the nurseries that once flourished in Hampton. Before the end of the nineteenth century much of the former farm land in the north-west of Hampton was converted to market gardens and nurseries. This area subsequently became the Nurserylands housing estate in the 1970s and '80s.

Local MP Sir Frederick Dixon-Hartland in 1906. He was Member of Parliament for the Uxbridge Division, which included Hampton, from 1885 until his death in 1909. He is seen here, the central figure with a light-coloured hat, campaigning with his wife, who is seated in the car. He scraped in, in this election, beating S.J. Pocock by 145 votes.

HAMPTON HILL

Park Road looking towards St James's Church, c. 1935, with recently pollarded trees lining the road. Note the old road sign on the left marking the crossroads with St James's Road. At one time there was a sharp bend in Park Road near a very narrow wooden bridge over the railway. This was eventually replaced by the present brick bridge and the road was straightened.

Tram passing over the Pantile Bridge, *c.* 1910. Previously a much narrower pantile bridge, dating from 1832, had existed with a watersplash alongside through which heavy traffic had to pass. After 1903 Hampton Hill High Street needed to be widened to accommodate double tram tracks instead of the original single track. This process started around 1907/8 and the new bridge opened in 1910.

Coronation festivities in honour of George V, 1911. The procession included decorated bicycles, delivery carts and horses, cars, fire engines and floats. The view is looking towards the Jenny Lind public house in the High Street which was built in 1839. The name comes from the famous singer, also known as 'The Swedish Nightingale', who first appeared on stage in London in 1837.

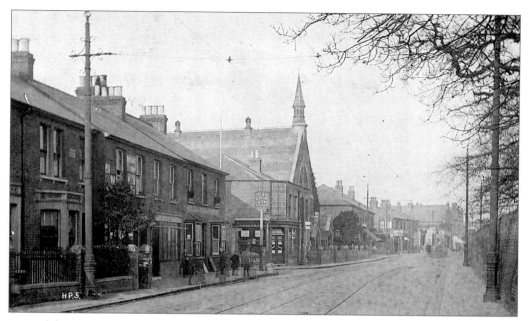

View of the High Street taken near the Rising Sun public house whose signboard can be seen outside, *c.* 1907. The Congregational Church (now the United Reformed Church) is in the centre of the picture. In those days the church had a miniature spire on the roof but this has now gone. However, apart from the tramlines, the scene is still fairly similar today.

Windmill Road, *c.* 1905, named after the windmill which used to stand opposite the present Windmill public house. The windmill had been built on what was then the common in 1785 and was demolished in 1876. The fire station was located in Windmill Road after the previous one, built in 1898 in High Street, was demolished to allow for road widening to take the trams.

A very unusual picture of the pasteurizing and cooling plant for J. Prewett and Sons taken in the 1920s. At this time cows were milked behind the shop in High Street, in milking sheds now converted to house electrical milk floats. Later the cows were kept at Chessington in Surrey. The dairy was subsequently taken over by Job's and, at a later date, by Unigate.

High Street with what was the Crown and Anchor public house on the left-hand side, c. 1940. The original Crown and Anchor was built c. 1823 and was replaced by the present building when the road was widened to take double tram tracks in 1907. Latterly the pub became the Valiant Knight and is now Joe's Restaurant. On the right-hand side can be seen the post office run by Mr Makepeace and subsequently his daughters from before the turn of the century until the 1940s.

F.W. Paines's butcher's shop, with a good display of meat, in High Street, *c.* 1913. The signboard claims that the business was established in 1818. Not only has pollution increased since those days but so has knowledge of hygiene – which would now prevent such a display!

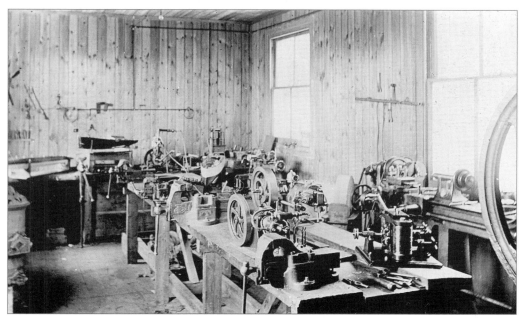

Metal workshop, Burlington House, *c.* 1915. An unusual interior view of a metal workshop in Burlington House at the time of the First World War.

View of the High Street looking towards Park Terrace, *c.* 1905. This picture gives some idea of the fine houses and gardens that lined High Street in the period, before extensive redevelopment and the construction of new shops.

Park Terrace, High Street, *c.* 1910. The first building on the left-hand side was then occupied by J.B. Howe and is now the premises of the Cavan Bakery. The railings and trees on the right-hand side conceal what were then commodious villas for the gentry on land which has now been redeveloped as Parkside.

The junction of Park Road and High Street well before the traffic lights were installed, *c.* 1915. The building on the left, which was then occupied by Jones and Peers who sold furnishings and were general ironmongers, now houses picture-framers and the Hampton Hill Gallery. A variety of interesting period costume is shown and an early pram stands outside the shop.

Group photograph of a charabanc outing taken outside the premises of Jones and Peers at the corner of Park Road and High Street, *c.* 1910. The vehicle is from J.J. Harper of Bell Garage, Hampton and the destination plate shows Hampton. The vehicle is a Daimler with solid tyres and the speed limit, printed on the side, is 12 m.p.h.

St James's Church, *c.* 1910. The church was consecrated in December 1863 and was originally a simple structure consisting of nave, chancel and vestry room. By 1876 the north and south aisle, porch and organ chamber had all been added and the chancel had been enlarged. The tower and spire were added in 1887 to celebrate Queen Victoria's Jubilee. Most of this work was inspired by the Revd Fitzroy John Fitzwygram who died in 1881.

St James's Sunday School Parade, 23 July 1908, pictured on a postcard belonging to the Job family. Charles Robert Job was the third vicar of St James's and the incumbent from 1893 to 1914. The first vicar had been the Revd Fitzroy John Fitzwygram, in post from 1863 until his early death in 1881. The second vicar was Henry Vesey Bligh, son of the Earl of Darnley, who held the position from 1881 until 1893.

High Street, c. 1925. The Duke of Clarence public house is on the left-hand side. The exact origins of the Duke of Clarence are not known – records show that it was one of three beer-houses existing in the area in 1850 (the others were The Crown and Anchor and The Duke of Wellington). The Duke of Clarence is believed to be on the site of an earlier building.

Fulwell and Hampton Hill Station, now Fulwell Station, *c.* 1907. The railway had reached Hampton in 1863 and this, as well as the building of the Hampton Waterworks from the late 1850s onwards, led to a great influx of workers into the area and the consequent growth of Hampton Hill. The railway also provided easy access to the market for nursery products and encouraged professional people to come to what had previously been considered an inaccessible area.

Fulwell Railway Bridge, 24 July 1902. The coming of the trams meant that much of the local road system including bridges had to be rebuilt. The laying of the tramlines had reached Fulwell Bridge by the end of 1902.

HAMPTON COURT

Pleasure boats moored near the riverbank beside Hampton Court Palace. The palace had been opened to the public by Queen Victoria in 1838 and initially most visitors came by the railway, which had reached Hampton Court in 1849, and from 1903 onwards many came by tram. On the other side of the river are some of the houseboats that used to be moored there.

View of the King's Arms Hotel, located beside the Lion Gate at Hampton Court, *c.* 1910. Records show that a King's Arms had occupied the site since the seventeenth century, although the present building dates from later. The King's Arms still serves a very large number of visitors today, as it has done for centuries past.

A view of the shops in Hampton Court Road, opposite the King's Arms Hotel and just down from the entrance to Bushy Park, *c.* 1910. The tall building was the Queen's Arms Inn (still standing but no longer an inn). On the extreme right were the premises of A. Togni and Son which provided teas and a dining room with 'grand views of Bushy Park'.

HAMPTON COURT.   The Most Charming Place to take AFTERNOON TEA.

On the LOVELY BALCONY TEA GARDENS
(Overlooking Bushey Park).
AFTERNOON TEAS Daintily Served at Popular Prices   Accommodation for 300.
LOOK FOR THE BIG WHITE FLAG.   PROPRIETOR: J. S. BURTON.

Balcony Tea Gardens, Hampton Court, *c.* 1910. This establishment was one of many around the fringes of Hampton Court and Bushy Park that specialized in teas and refreshments. Many of the visitors catered for came by bicycle, train or riverboat in the days before the widespread use of the motor car.

The Whitehall Hotel, opposite Hampton Court Green during the First World War. At this time the premises were also known as the Whitehall Auxiliary Military Hospital. Later the building was used as the Bearstead Memorial Hospital and more recently as a home for the elderly, Rotary Court.

A view of the bridge approach and old (third) bridge at Hampton Court with the Mitre Hotel on the right-hand side, *c.* 1925. The first bridge existed from 1753 to 1778, the second from 1778 to 1864, the third (shown here) from 1865 until 1933. The present bridge was opened by HRH the Prince of Wales on 3 July 1933. The Mitre was in existence in the seventeenth century, although it occupied an earlier building.

The third bridge at Hampton Court, *c.* 1905. Its brick-built approaches can still be seen on both sides of the river, as can the old toll house on the Middlesex side which is now incorporated as part of the Mitre Hotel. The fourth and present bridge was built slightly downstream from the one shown here and its construction involved the demolition of the Castle Hotel which had stood since around 1620.

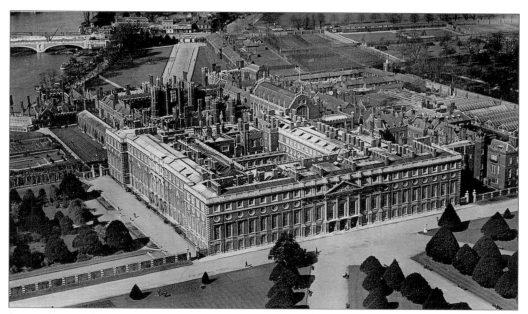

An aerial view of Hampton Court Palace, *c.* 1933. Careful examination of Hampton Court Bridge (top left) shows a crane building the new bridge and the old bridge alongside it. This view shows clearly the south and east fronts, with Fountain Court in the middle, which were constructed by Sir Christopher Wren for William and Mary in the period 1689–1702.

The Tudor Moat Bridge leading to the main west front gateway was excavated in 1909/10. Built in 1535 the bridge was covered up *c.* 1689 and the moat filled in. Thus the moat and Moat Bridge were 'lost' for some 220 years (from 1689 until 1909). After excavation in 1909 copies of the Tudor heraldic King's beasts were placed in position in 1911, on each side of the bridge.

The Tudor Kitchens were built by Wolsey and extended by Henry VIII. The demands on the kitchens were enormous. The Great Hall sat about 300 people and there had to be two sittings as about 600 people were entitled to eat there. After enlargement by Henry the kitchens comprised over fifty rooms covering 36,000 square feet.

The Great Vine at Hampton Court, planted in 1768 and seen here *c.* 1910. In the past it has produced more than 2,000 lb of grapes in a single year, but now fewer bunches are allowed to grow to maturity.

ACKNOWLEDGEMENTS

In the preparation of this book we have received much help and support from friends and colleagues and in particular we would like to thank Vic Rosewarne for some of the pictures of Whitton and the corresponding text, likewise Alan Urwin, Donald Simpson and E.A. Morris for some of the pictures of Twickenham. Thanks are also due to David Senior, the Bristol Record Office and the Curator (Photographic Archives) of the National Tramways Museum for some of the early transport pictures. As usual Chris Turfitt and Jane Baxter of the Local Studies section of Twickenham Library have given us much-needed support and the London Borough of Richmond has provided several of our subject pictures. Colin Pain has kindly made available his wealth of knowledge on Hampton Wick and Tony Cannings expertly copied some pictures loaned to us. Dick Cashmore and Tony Beckles Willson offered their help and advice in several areas. Jill Ross discovered the picture of Teddington Fire Brigade. Finally, Sharman Sheaf undertook the difficult task of transcribing her husband's notes to give us a legible copy of the Hampton captions.

FURTHER READING

BOTLHS denotes Borough of Twickenham Local History Society

Alford, Maud, *Mrs Alford Remembers – Twickenham in the 1880s* (BOTLHS 21), 1986.

Anstead, C.M. and Heath, G.D., *Bushy Park – Victorian Playground of the People* (BOTLHS 4), 1965.

Atkins, Frank, *A Short Guide to the Parish Church of St Mary the Virgin*, various editions.

Beckles Willson, Anthony, *Mr Pope and Others at Cross Deep, Twickenham in the Eighteenth Century*, 1996.

Beckles Willson, Anthony, *Strawberry Hill – A History of the Neighbourhood*, 1991.

Borough of Twickenham Local History Society, *Twickenham 1600–1900: People and Places* (BOTLHS 47), 1981.

Borough of Twickenham Local History Society, *Twickenham As It Was* (Hendon), 1982.

Borough of Twickenham Local History Society, *Old Hampton, Hampton Hill and Hampton Wick* (Hendon), 1982.

Borough of Twickenham Local History Society, *Bygone Twickenham* (Hendon), 1983.

Bunch, Maureen, *Cambridge Park, Twickenham and its Owners 1616–1835* (BOTLHS 63), 1989.

Bunch, Maureen, *Cambridge Park East Twickenham, The Building of a Suburb* (BOTLHS 68), 1992.

Cashmore, T.H.R., *High Shot House – The Story of a Twickenham Villa* (BOTLHS 32), 1975.

Cashmore, T.H.R., *York House Twickenham* (BOTLHS Occasional Paper 4), 1990.

Chaplin, Peter, *The Thames at Hampton*, 1967.

Ching, Pamela, *Teddington in 1800 – The Year of the Enclosure* (BOTLHS 51), 1983.

Ching, Pamela, *The History of the Roads of Teddington* (Teddington Society), 1989.

Garside, Bernard, *A Brief History of Hampton School, 1557–1957*, 1957.

Gascoigne, Bamber and Ditchburn, Jonathan, *Images of Twickenham*, St Helena Press, 1981.

Heath, Gerald, *The Formation of the Local Boards of Twickenham, Teddington, Hampton and Hampton Wick* (BOTLHS 10), 1967.

Heath, Gerald, *Hampton in the Nineteenth Century* (BOTLHS 27), 1993, 2nd edn.

Howe, Ken, *Teddington – Past and Present* (Hendon), 1994.

Law, Ernest, *A Short History of Hampton Court*, 1st edn, 1897.

McCutcheon Nelson, Helen and Pearce, Brian Louis, *The Happiest Days . . . A History of Education in Twickenham 1645–1918* (BOTLHS 70), 1994.

McCutcheon Nelson, Helen, *The Happiest Days . . . A History of Education in Twickenham Part II: Twentieth-century Schools* (BOTLHS 73), 1995.

Orton, Margery (ed.), *The Birth and Growth of Hampton Hill*, 1965.

Ripley, Henry, *The History and Topography of Hampton-on-Thames*, 1883.

Sandford, R., *Excavations in Church Street* (BOTLHS 12), 1968.

Sheaf, John and Howe, Ken, *Hampton and Teddington Past* (Historical Publications), 1995.

Simpson, D.H. and Morris, E.A., *Twickenham Ferries in History and Song* (BOTLHS 43), 1980.

Simpson, Donald, *Twickenham Past* (Historical Publications), 1993.

Thames Valley Times, various issues

Thurley, Simon, *Hampton Court Palace Souvenir Guide, 2nd edn, 1992.*

Urwin, Alan, *Twickenham Park, 1965.*

Urwin, Alan, *Railshead, 1974.*

Urwin, Alan, Commercial Nurseries and Market Gardens (BOTLHS 50), 1982.

Urwin, Alan, *The Manor House Twickenham* (BOTLHS 60), 1987.

Victoria County History of Middlesex, *Vols* II *and* III.

Wallis, Dorothy, *St John's Hospital — The Early Years* (BOTLHS 14), 1969.

Yates, Edward, *Hampton Court, 1935.*

INDEX

T W I C K E N H A M A N D W H I T T O N

INDEX

TEDDINGTON, HAMPTON WICK AND BUSHY PARK

INDEX

HAMPTON, HAMPTON HILL AND HAMPTON COURT